Modern Art in Prints
Riva Castleman

The Museum of Modern Art, New York

Copyright © 1973 by The Museum of Modern Art
All rights reserved
Library of Congress Catalog Card Number 72-95073
ISBN 0-87070-461-3
Designed by James Wageman
Type set by AR Typographers, Inc.
Printed by Scroll Press, Inc., Danbury, Connecticut
The Museum of Modern Art
11 West 53 Street, New York, New York 10019
Printed in the United States of America

Contents

This book has been published
in conjunction with an exhibition
organized under the auspices of
The International Council of
The Museum of Modern Art.

Acknowledgments

The prints illustrated in this book were selected for an exhibition that was formed for circulation in Asia, New Zealand, and Australia. More than half of the prints were collected by The International Council of The Museum of Modern Art, under whose auspices the exhibition has been organized. A few prints from the Collection of The Museum of Modern Art are also included. On behalf of the Museum and The International Council I wish to express appreciation to Mr. and Mrs. Robert Dain, New York; Mr. S. I. Newhouse, Jr., New York; Reiss-Cohen, Inc., New York; David Whitney, New York; The National Gallery of Art, Washington, D. C.; and one anonymous lender, who generously made works available for the extensive tour of the exhibition.

For their invaluable advice and encouragement I am most grateful to William S. Lieberman, Chief Curator of Drawings, and Waldo Rasmussen, Director of the International Program. I wish also to thank Antoinette King, Senior Paper Conservator, for her knowledgeable essay on the care of prints; Barbara London, Program Assistant, for her aid in preparing the exhibition; Mrs. Susan Wolf, Editor; and James Wageman, Senior Designer.

R.C.

Color Plates

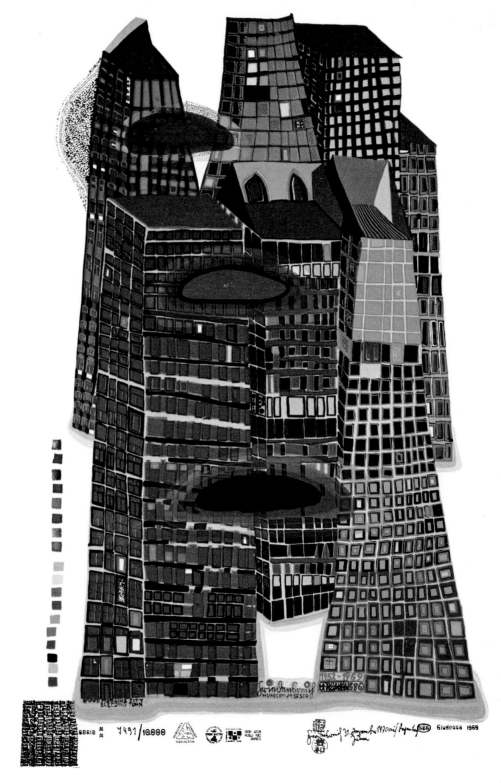

52/100   Soulages

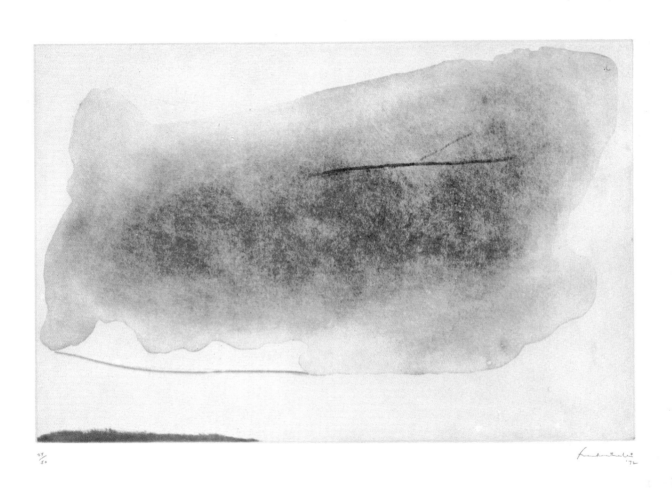

24/50   Frankenthaler '72

13

K.

A. Vermont

J. The World

E. Wank

D. Köln

B. Syracuse

C. Chez Myx

F. Utland

G. Ohio

H. Havana

hearts.

I. St. Louis

14

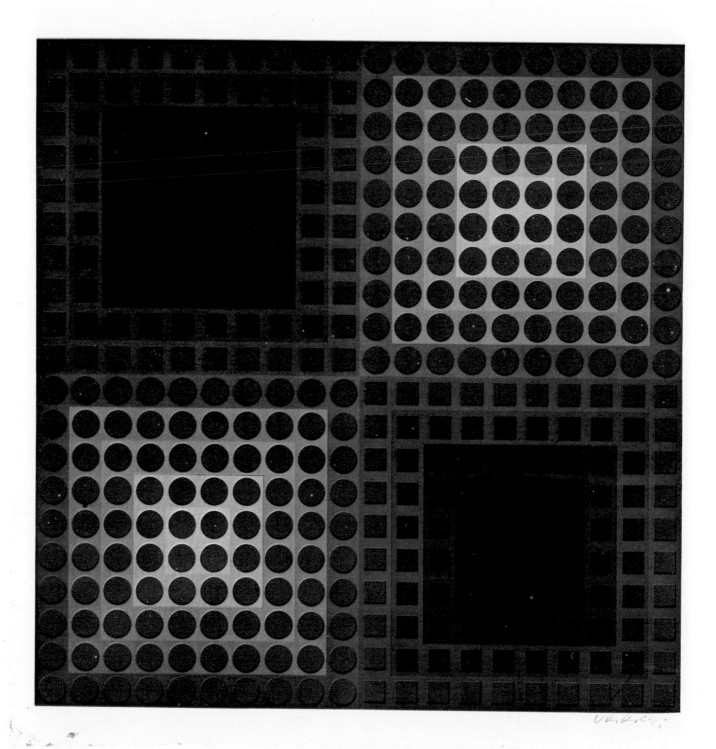

16

Modern Art in Prints

Introduction

In order to survey the history of Western, that is, European and American, printmaking during the last quarter-century one would need to represent works by literally thousands of artists. This small selection of fifty prints is therefore but a hint at some of the more potent stylistic developments in art during the period. The writer has included examples of various technical approaches to printmaking that have altered traditional concepts, but makes no attempt to show in depth the work of one artist or even of one school. This is, rather, a condensed view of contemporary printmaking, designed to offer an awareness of the foundations upon which the art of our time is building.

World War II had an unsettling effect upon the entire world. It precipitated the dissemination of Western culture into the most remote areas. Technological developments created a network of communications that allowed ideas and men to move rapidly and freely. The historian Arnold J. Toynbee wrote in 1947, "Future historians will say, I think, that the great event of the twentieth century was the impact of the Western Civilization upon all the other living societies of the world of that day. They will say of this impact that it was so powerful and so pervasive that it turned the lives of all its victims upside down and inside out—affecting the behavior, outlook, feelings, and beliefs of individual men, women, and children in an intimate way, touching chords in human souls that are not touched by mere external forces—however ponderous and terrifying." He expected the profound religion-like conversion of mankind into a single social unit. The attractiveness of Western ideas and means has been modified by a renewed awareness in the East of the merits of tradition, and most recently the passage of ideas has become reciprocal. Because barriers of language rarely exist in the visual arts, the Oriental assimilation of Western forms has been rapid. The continuing revelation to both the East and the West of art as a product of a complex past responding to present and future needs may indeed create unique growth and vision.

During the past twenty-five years humanity has lived through the infancy of the atomic and space ages. This has been an era in which man's recognition of his own destructive powers has permeated society with fear, aggravated by continual conflict in all parts of the world. Although this fear and the frustration that accompanies it occasionally surface in art, by and large the artist's imagination carries his work, tangential to social concerns, into the realm of the undiscovered and unexplored. A direct reaction to a contemporary event, as in Picasso's *Guernica,* occasionally occurs in art, but contemporary life-styles seem to have deeper influences. Sensitive to the daily events that shift the moods of society, the artist has seen postwar affluence and created pop art, and has observed the general reverence for science and logic and invented conceptual art.

Stylistic trends in art throughout the postwar years have ranged from European abstraction and the New York school of abstract expressionism, pop art, new figuration, and op art to conceptual art and neo-realism. These names, however, are overlapping tags that rarely cover adequately what they attempt to isolate and define. There is no definitive chronological order in this book except in parts where it emerges naturally from the progression of certain movements. The problem of sequence is further complicated by the facts that many developments have taken place simultaneously and that many of the prints illustrated here were made well after the genesis of these developments. The prints are thus grouped aesthetically— to show, as much as possible, parallel developments in manners of viewing the contemporary environment and of executing a work of art.

The selection of prints begins with several works by European painters who had attained their stylistic maturity long before World War II. Favorable response to their postwar prints created a larger audience for works in various print media. More painters and sculptors began to make prints, and new techniques, particularly in the areas of intaglio and relief printing, were extensively developed.

Lithography was the process that appealed to most artists, and their interest led to a revival of that medium in both Europe and the United States of America. Lithography depended upon the collaboration of the artist with the printer and led to close working relationships and the production of great quantities of prints. Many artists of the 1960's whose paintings tended to have sharp edges and vivid colors utilized serigraph (also called silkscreen or screenprinting) and made it an important medium. Its development paralleled the acceptance of photographic techniques and images into the fine arts.

Much too often during the past twenty-five years the question of the originality of artists' prints has drawn attention away from their aesthetic value. Definitions which attempted to differentiate between an original print and a reproduction of a unique work such as a painting rarely have taken into account more than the protection of the consumer. The artist's physical limitations generally characterize the unique works that come from his hand, such as drawings and paintings. In this age of micrometers the impossibility of the same hand exactly duplicating its own work is readily acknowledged. Even so, a tool intervenes between the artist's hand and the surface upon which he creates art: a pencil, a pen, a brush. In the case of unique works the chain from hand to canvas or paper is two links long: the brush and paint, the pencil and lead, the pen and ink. The longer and more complex the chain is, the better the possibility for duplication. When an artist intends to make a print, one of the several multiple art forms, he prepares to pick up one link in a chain that may branch many times before the image he has conceived appears on paper. Depending on the complexity of the medium and the artist's working attitude, there are varying amounts of direct application of the tools of printmaking that the artist may undertake. However, at the end, when the image is printed, the artist must acknowledge that this is his intended work of art. Since the nineteenth century this has been done by having the artist sign and number each print in the edition (total number of images printed). This has led to certain conformities in the format of the original print which have confined the artist's expression in many cases and have often led to revolt. The more certain the artist is that his image and the print medium he has chosen are inseparable, the more original and successful his print will be.

In order to use this book effectively the reader should keep a finger in the index. For a systematic understanding of print media, the reader will find references in conjunction with typical examples. This will not always occur in the first text that refers to a print in a particular medium. Sections in the text have been devoted to two printmaking techniques: intaglio and relief. The majority of the prints, however, are lithographs and are not similarly isolated.

A supplement on the care and preservation of prints on paper is included for those who own prints already or who wish to begin collecting this form of original art.

Readers are begged to keep their eyes on the prints as much as possible. All the titles, dates, artists' biographies, historical facts, and technical data cannot vivify a work of art that does not live in the viewer's eye.

Where no collection is mentioned in the caption for a print, the work is owned by The International Council of The Museum of Modern Art. Unless otherwise noted, the dimensions given are plate or composition size, height preceding width. A date is enclosed in parentheses when it does not appear on the work.

Marc Chagall French, born Russia 1889
Kamaralkamara Elopes with the Princess on the Ebony Horse. Plate XII from *Four Tales from the Arabian Nights*. (1948), Pantheon, New York.
Color lithograph, 14⅞ x 11⅜".
The Museum of Modern Art, New York (gift of Albert Carman).

Marc Chagall created his first color lithographs as illustrations for *Four Tales from the Arabian Nights*. As was his custom, he began by making gouaches of his subjects. These were later translated into the graphic media with the aid of a master printer. The brilliant colors of the *Arabian Nights* lithographs are built up by overprinting transparent pastel inks. The result of the printer's work was a lithographic crayon and wash version of the gouaches, a traditional approach in which the artist's role in printmaking is limited. Chagall approved the printed versions of the gouache compositions and added areas of color and other corrective marks. Not being a craftsman in what is a considerably sophisticated medium, Chagall used lithography as a means of extending and varying an image made in a different medium.

The prints for the *Arabian Nights* were executed while Chagall was in exile in New York because of the Second World War. He had designed the decor and costumes for Stravinsky's ballet *Firebird* in 1945, and the Oriental splendor of those designs continues in his illustrations for Sheherezade's fantastic tales. The subject of the print is the story of "The Ebony Horse," or "The Enchanted Horse," and illustrates the following text: "Mounting the ebony horse he took her up behind him and made her fast to himself, binding her with strong bonds; after which he turned the shoulder-pin of ascent, and the horse rose with him in air. . . ." The united lovers, Chagall's favorite theme since his Russian youth, are enveloped by the magic blue void as they fly to their happy ending.

André Masson   French, born 1896
Lake Como. Plate 2 from *Voyage à Venise.*
(1950–1951), Galerie Louise Leiris, Paris.
Color lithograph, 15-13/16 x 12-7/16".
The Museum of Modern Art, New York
(the Celeste and Armand Bartos Fund).

Lithography is based on the mutual antipathy
between grease and water. Special Bavarian
limestones and treated zinc and aluminum plates
are drawn upon with a greasy crayon or liquid
(tusche), lightly etched with gum acid so that only
the image will accept the ink, and kept wet so that
the natural inclination of the stone or plate to accept
grease or ink will be forestalled. Ink is rolled onto
the dampened surface, paper placed over it, and
both are run through a flatbed press under
considerable pressure.

André Masson, like Chagall, did not at first work
directly on the stone when he made lithographs.
This transfer lithograph was first drawn in black
crayon on a sheet of special paper, and the drawn
image was then transferred to the stone. Unlike most
color lithographs, which require a separate stone or
plate for each color desired, this print was taken
from one stone on which the several colors were
applied very carefully. Because there is no overlapping of color, the image is broken up by the
discreet areas of color as well as by the quick,
regular crayon strokes of a sketch made directly
from nature.

This lithograph is from an album of forty prints
that documents a trip Masson made to Venice in
1950. He was in the neighboring area during early
fall, and describes his stop at Lake Como: "The air
one breathes there is like azure, and day and night
it is a complete gamut of the most delicate and
tender blues. We don't exhaust the vocabulary. However, quite simply we agree that it is enchanting...."

Pablo Picasso   Spanish, born 1881
Owl on a Chair. (1947), Louise Leiris, Paris.
Color lithograph, 25½ x 19½".
National Gallery of Art, Washington, D. C.
(International Art Foundation).

When World War II was over, life in Paris was perhaps more confused and difficult than it had been during the Nazi occupation. There was a shortage of fuel and despite his affluence and fame, Pablo Picasso also lacked heat. He found a warm refuge in the lithography workshop of Fernand Mourlot. Mourlot's printers worked on bottle labels and reproductions of paintings as well as artist's prints, and Picasso first visited the shop when Mourlot requested permission to reproduce some of his paintings. With the concentrated energy that he has applied to all his work, Picasso threw himself into the creation of lithographs. He utilized all the techniques he could and developed new ones only because he would not stop working long enough to learn the traditional ways of making a lithograph.

This crayon lithograph is one of Picasso's rare compositions that contains no people. The owl, however, was a constant companion in his household during this period. After he began to spend more time in southern France, where owls of several varieties abound, they were often the subjects of his ceramics. For Picasso, a native of the Mediterranean shore, the owl is, with the faun, the centaur, and the minotaur, a natural symbol in the area once inhabited by the ancient Greeks and populated with their mythology.

Fernand Léger   French, 1881–1955
Composition from *Brunidor, Album 2.*
(1948), Brunidor Editions, New York.
Color lithograph, 15¾ x 10-13/16".
The Museum of Modern Art, New York.

Like Chagall, Fernand Léger spent the years during World War II in the United States of America. There he caught the spirit of the American circus which was to be the basis of one of his most extensive series of paintings and the subject of a book he wrote and illustrated in 1950. Many of his compositions combined forms of evident machine manufacture with elements of nature such as roots, sunflowers, and cacti. These were parts of a newly discovered landscape that both intrigued him and allowed him to pursue the evolution of his monumental style.

The presence in New York of many prominent European artists encouraged their admirers to conceive programs that would take advantage of such creative abundance. Several commissioned prints. Typical of this activity was the publication program of Brunidor Editions. In the first Brunidor Portfolio etchings and lithographs by Max Ernst, Matta, and Miró appeared. This lithograph by Léger was included in the second album, which was finally issued in 1952. The composition of solid rocklike clouds filling the spaces between patterned strips, flattened spirals, and a coglike form, all derived from machine elements, is one of the few lithographs of the period that sparkles with color.

Léger's manner of making lithographs was in the French tradition. He would draw the black outline either directly on the lithographic stone or on transfer paper. After the proof of that drawing was printed, he would fill in the color on the proof. From this the printer would make the separate plates for each color. When the printer was able to duplicate the hand-colored proof in his trial proof, the artist would either suggest corrections or approve it for printing *(bon à tirer)*.

Henri Matisse   French, 1869–1954
The Nightmare of the White Elephant from *Jazz.*
(1947), Tériade, Paris.
Color pochoir, 16-3/16 x 25⅛".
The Museum of Modern Art, New York (gift of the
artist).

The most colorful works to emerge in the form of
prints during the 1940's were the illustrations Henri
Matisse made for his book *Jazz.* They were first
executed as cutouts from painted papers, the
process Matisse used most often after he had
become almost completely bedridden in the early
1940's. Stencils made after the forms of the cutouts
were printed with the paints Matisse originally used
to color his paper cutouts. The paint was applied
through the stencil with brushes, the oldest manner
of stencil printing, known by its French name *pochoir.*
The colors are, therefore, more brilliant than any
printer's ink could convey. In their unsubtle, bright,
opaque paints the prints of *Jazz* forecast the
popularity of silkscreen, the stencil technique
preferred by most of the pop artists of the 1960's.

The subjects of the *Jazz* illustrations "resulted
from crystallizations of memories of the circus,
popular tales, or of travel," according to Matisse's
text. Here the performing white circus elephant
stands precariously on a ball surrounded by a nightmare of the unfamiliar. Red slashes menace his
stability while black wave/leaf forms could well be
his threatening audience. These forms and use of
color are the essence of Matisse's late work.
[See color plate, page 9.]

Georges Braque   French, 1882–1963
Leaves, Color, Light. (1953), Aimé Maeght, Paris
Color lithograph, 38-3/16 x 23-13/16".
National Gallery of Art, Washington, D.C.
(International Art Foundation).

The majority of the compositions of Georges Braque
were based upon the exploration of one subject,
still life. All but one of his earliest prints of 1908–
1912 were still lifes in the cubist manner. In 1945,
when Braque began a long series of lithographs at
the workshop of Fernand Mourlot in Paris, the
chances were that most of the prints would be still
lifes. Seven years later, after developing a fine sense
for the medium, Braque completed the lithograph
Leaves, Color, Light, one of the outstanding works
to appear during the postwar revival of color
lithography.

The tendency of other artists to use a brush and
tusche in a painterly way in lithography generally
results in prints that should have been paintings.
Braque astutely surrounded areas he wished to
remain white with absolutely flat areas of color,
increasing the visual contrast; volume is conveyed
by pale washes, and a sense of depth results from
overprintings of transparent colors. Braque's intro-
duction of a black margin that both frames and is
part of the composition, as well as the unusually
large size of the sheet, extended the role of the print
further into the arena of wall object, where it would
compete with painting. There were few lithographs
before this one that so well incorporated the
possibilities of the medium and anticipated the
future role of the print in the 1960's.

Jean Arp French, 1887–1966
Configuration. (1951), Guilde Internationale de la Gravure, Paris.
Color lithograph, 20-3/16 x 12".
The Museum of Modern Art, New York (Larry Aldrich Fund).

Jean Arp, one of the first and least bombastic of the dadaists, was a poet and an artist. From the time of World War I until his death in 1966, he worked methodically on abstract (he preferred the word "concrete") forms that had their basis in nature. Although he later made sculpture in the round, he began in 1914 to make wood reliefs that were constructions of flat shapes glued onto a board. The wood was often painted in contrasting colors that emphasized the floating, transcendent quality of the forms. He also made prints that could well have been printed from the reliefs, had he chosen to do so.

This lithograph is a two-dimensional translation of the type of biomorphic shape that appears in Arp's reliefs. The two forms are like amoebae, deriving direction and motion from their centers. A sense of shallow depth is also conveyed by the positive and negative renderings of the nuclei of the undulating organisms. Arp applied the title *Configuration* to both his visual art and poetry. In most of his visual configurations the primary form surrounds or is penetrated by a smaller one.

The first decade after World War II witnessed a growing interest in prints and printmaking techniques. Arp's lithograph was issued by the Guilde Internationale de la Gravure, an organization that commissioned, published, and distributed the prints of well-known artists. Because lithography was the most stable and accepted medium, the majority of the prints offered were lithographs even though, as in Arp's case, it was not always the artist's customary print medium. The next print, also issued by the Guilde, shows the extent to which technical developments were to affect the character of the traditional print.

Stanley William Hayter   British, born 1901
Sun Dance. (1951), Guilde Internationale de la
Gravure, Paris.
Color engraving and soft ground etching, 15½ x 9¾".
The Museum of Modern Art, New York (gift of Abby
Aldrich Rockefeller).

Formerly a chemist and geologist, Stanley William
Hayter began to make etchings in 1926. His scientific bent led him to experiment with the known
etching techniques and develop others. Hayter
revived the term intaglio (*intagliàre:* to cut into,
Italian) to cover the wealth of new techniques he
used. In intaglio prints (engraving, etching, aquatint,
soft ground, and so on) the image is always below
the original surface of the plate, either cut into it
(engraving and drypoint) or bitten into it by acid
(etching and aquatint). To print the plate, ink is
rubbed into those lower areas, generally wiped away
from the original surface, and the plate and a sheet
of dampened paper are put through a press.

Hayter's studio was open to artists who wished to
learn and experiment, and in 1933 he established
Atelier 17, where Giacometti and several of the
surrealist artists made their first prints. Besides
having an exceptional knowledge of technique,
Hayter was concerned with the surrealist's idea of
automatism, that is, allowing the pencil or other
instrument to wander over a surface without conscious guidance. During the forties and fifties, he
would begin a composition by taking the engraving
tool (burin) and cut into the plate without consider-
ing any form of composition. The technique is to
push the burin away from the body while the free
hand turns the plate, so the groove may continue
in any direction.

After engraving these automatic lines, Hayter
would search for a subject in them and, as in the
print *Sun Dance,* use diverse techniques to detail a
figure or group of figures. Quite often he would cut
deeply into the plate, which would emboss the paper
when the print was made. Textures were introduced
by means of soft ground, a varnish put over the
plate which remains soft and will expose the plate
when a material is pressed into it. In *Sun Dance,*
Hayter pressed a wood grain into the ground. Its
image remained permanently bitten into the plate
after it was put into acid.

Pierre Courtin French, born 1921
Composition. February 29, 1956.
Color engraving, 8-13/16 x 9-13/16″.
The Museum of Modern Art, New York
(gift of Theodore Schempp).

The idea of creating a modeled surface by means of impressing paper with deeply engraved plates or reliefs of hard materials is older than printmaking, having grown out of the use of seals. Over the centuries embossed paper has been used for official documents and decoration. During the 1930's Rolf Nesch and S. W. Hayter began making prints from collages of metal and screening and from perforated and deeply grooved metal plates. They molded areas of flat paper into low relief by printing their works under great pressure.

The engravings of Pierre Courtin differ from the above in that he usually cuts into the total surface of his zinc plate, modeling it into a thin relief, textured by tooling. Like the goldsmith, whose tools he uses, he shapes his metal into both hollow and raised areas. To obtain the stability of paper necessary for the retention of the relief, Courtin runs several sheets through the press together, simultaneously printing the image and laminating the paper. He generally inks his plates with several colors, wiping them together to obtain the worn effect that transforms his printed reliefs into evocations of strangely eroded ancient walls.

Lucio Fontana   Italian, 1899–1968
Spatial Concept. 1968, International Graphic Arts
Society, New York.
Etching, punctured, 25⅜ x 19".
The Museum of Modern Art, New York
(gift of International Graphic Arts Society, Inc.).

Shortly before his death the Italian artist Lucio
Fontana made this etching. It is related to the
paintings and an earlier series of etchings that he
described as spatial concepts. From 1948 on, the
combination of two compositional elements, an
enclosing line and punctured surface, was Fontana's
stylistic signature. In this print the line is a heavy
incrustation of ink, which stands up in sculptural
relief from the smooth, blackened surface of the
paper.

While the creation of prints with considerable
relief has become characteristic of the work of
intaglio printmakers during the past quarter of a
century, and paper has been molded into the holes
and gullies cut into copper plates, few printmakers
have achieved the drama of Fontana's print. Rather
than contorting the paper he has allowed it to
rupture, a physical destruction equivalent to his act
of perforating canvas. The punctured surface also
releases the planar tension established by the
restraining encircling line. In his efforts to make his
audience aware of the death of the traditional
painting Fontana created canvases with a single
powerful slash through them. The holes in this print
are equally vicious in their irreverent destruction of
the treasured integrity of paper.

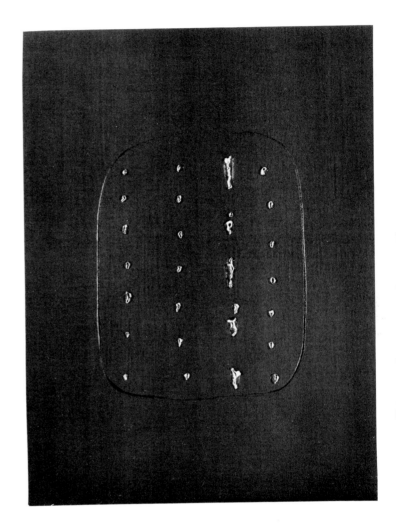

Omar Rayo   Colombian, born 1928
The Little Machine. (1963).
Inkless intaglio, 16⅜ x 7″.

Another method of heightening awareness of the materials of printmaking is seen in this uninked print by Omar Rayo. The heavy textured paper has been pressed with small smooth tools into grooves etched into a metal plate. Unlike traditional embossing, which requires positive and negative plates and flattens the texture of the paper in all areas where the two plates meet, Rayo's repoussé technique transforms only the areas where he has forced the pliable paper into the shapes he has devised. The result is a white, low relief in which shallow cast shadows of both the image and the untouched texture of the paper draw more than usual attention to the paper.

Rayo's subject matter has tended to focus this awareness. Generally he is concerned with ordinary objects: a book of matches, a glove, clothes hangers. In this case, *The Little Machine* is the very common safety pin, a form that Rayo has used in his prints many times and has also called *My First Hero.* Rayo's prints embody a sense of satire that might be considered a reflection of Latin American tradition. His paper reliefs of common objects transformed by scale and by the mystic purity of white seem to mock the customary respect for durable, monumental sculpture. Rayo's monuments of the ordinary contemporary things we depend upon are made of fragile, unenduring paper.

Leonard Baskin   American, born 1922
The Anatomist. 1952.
Color woodcut, 18¾ x 11″.

After World War II the art of woodcut, the oldest of
the printing media, was revived internationally.
Collectors and critics took new interest in the works
of the German expressionists of the first quarter of
the twentieth century, most of whom had been
labeled degenerate by the Nazis and who gave
vitality to the old craft. Some artists again turned
to the folk sources that had been so influential in the
earlier movement. Another approach was Leonard
Baskin's: He combined the directness of the
expressionists with the elegant precision of the
sixteenth-century woodcutter. The artistic aims and
mannerisms of the English mystic artist William
Blake and the German sculptor Ernst Barlach also
were important influences.

Baskin's subject matter is often literary, arising
from his interest in the illustrated books of past
centuries. The anatomical studies of Vesalius, for
example, have been the source for the freely inter-
preted, cadaver-like representation Baskin favors.
A tense linear web alludes to the musculature of the
figure as well as the weave of the cloth covering it.
This print is one of several woodcuts that Baskin
created in the early 1950's to represent a search for
the image of man through classic forms: the univer-
sality of *Everyman,* the tragedy of *Haman,* the
scientific objectivity of *The Anatomist.* In each is the
hint of moral corruption, the human imperfection
that has its basis in the Judaic tradition which
pervades Baskin's work.

Baskin's method of woodcutting in this print is
classical, the image remaining in sharp relief from
the areas of the woodblock that have been removed
with a gouge or knife. Though this print is in two
colors, the areas of black and red are isolated from
each other so that it was possible to put both colors
of ink on the block simultaneously and complete the
work in one printing.

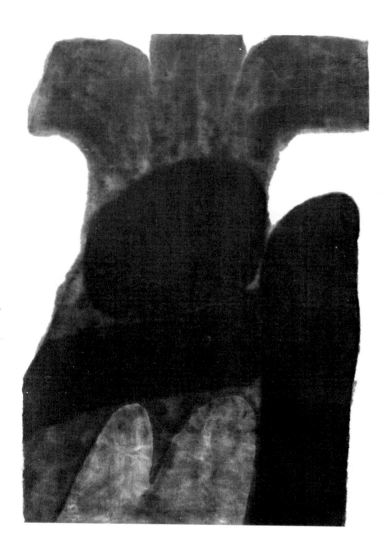

Carol Summers   American, born 1925
Stromboli Dark. 1965.
Color woodcut, 29¼ x 21".

Another artist who was influenced by the revival of
interest in the woodcuts of artists such as Paul
Gauguin and Edvard Munch was the American Carol
Summers. He began to cut his woodblocks in the
traditional manner but found himself more interested
in the behavior of ink than in the texture of wood.
At that point in the 1950's he was combining stencil
and woodblocks to change the densities and distri-
bution of the ink on the thin Japan paper customarily
used to print woodcuts. Eventually he developed the
method used for *Stromboli Dark*. It is perhaps closer
to stencil and rubbing techniques than to woodcut.
Summers cuts out plywood forms in the shapes he
desires for each color or compositional element. He
places his paper over the uninked form and applies
the ink directly to the paper, using a paint solvent to
dilute and spread the color beyond the area
supported by the cut wood form. For more opaque
colors Summers prints a flat, nonporous white on
the verso of the paper to prevent the ink from
soaking through.

The fresh, autographic appearance of Summers's
woodcuts comes from the spread of ink through the
uneven silk fibers of the paper. This quality, derived
from the freer style of Oriental ink drawing that
appealed to Western taste of this time, depends
upon complete but not inhibiting control of the
printing materials. Through the use of ink alone
Summers has managed to convey the awesome
appearance of a dormant but ominous volcano.

Eduardo Chillida Spanish, born 1924
Ikur. (1972), Aimé Maeght, Paris.
Woodcut, 30 x 21⅞".

While the previous example of woodcut alters the concept of how a print from wood should appear, the inherent quality of the material of the block is masked by an innovative use of ink. In this print by the Spanish sculptor Eduardo Chillida, there is no doubt that hard, resistant blocks of wood have been impressed on paper. Chillida often creates sculpture from milled wood and extruded metal. These already processed materials of forms made familiar by their use in the construction of functional objects are transformed into sculpture by the unfamiliar conjunction of their shapes.

Chillida's sculptures are generally formed of interlocking parts and, like the constructed chain of blocks in this print, represent his individual approach to the delimitation of space. In the print the connected blocks continue beyond the confines of the paper's edge. Their insertion into space is indefinite; we are only able to define the chain of blocks by its intrusion onto a sheet of textured paper. Although we could guess that the print is a partial documentation of a sculpture under these circumstances, it is the artist's refined use of the relief printing technique of woodcut that conveys this impression.

Pablo Picasso   Spanish, born 1881
Picador and Bullfighter. (1959), Louise Leiris, Paris.
Color linoleum cut, 21 x 25¼".
Reiss-Cohen, Inc., New York.

Picasso, too, has made unique contributions to the expansion of printmaking methods. The processes that have been described so far have been predominantly embellishments or variations on traditional techniques. Photography was ignored by the artists or publishers of these prints, and sophisticated machinery was consciously avoided, largely because of the customary hand and craft orientation of painting and sculpture. Virtuosity alone affected the look of the well-exploited print media. In this area Picasso has had no peer.

No longer wishing to visit the Parisian lithography and etching workshops after settling in southern France, Picasso looked for a new place to create prints. In Vallauris he found Arnéra, a craftsman who printed linoleum cut posters. Picasso began to make posters in this rather innocuous, homogenous material. As he grew older, he had less and less patience with the time-consuming processes of proofing and registering the separate blocks for each color. With Arnéra, Picasso made one last seven-block print in which the failure to register exactly dominated the image. At that point Picasso decided on a means to assure perfect registration: He cut all the colors successively from one linoleum block. This procedure—cutting the block, printing it in an amount larger than the anticipated edition, recutting the same block and printing it in another color over the already printed sheets, cutting again and printing again—left no opportunity for mistakes.

The print shown here was made from a block first printed without any cuts in a solid light color, then cut and printed in a second color, and cut once more and printed in black. Depicted is one of Picasso's favorite subjects, a scene from the bullfight. The arching contours of the horse and bullfighter as well as the sparkling gouges that vivify and decorate the larger masses result from and are intrinsic to the linoleum material. [See color plate, page 10.]

Jean Dubuffet   French, born 1901
Carrot Nose. 1962.
Color lithograph, 23-13/16 x 14⅞".
The Museum of Modern Art, New York
(gift of Mr. and Mrs. Ralph F. Colin).

His interest in naïve and insane art, often created out of simple but unconventional materials, undoubtedly contributed to the development of Jean Dubuffet's personal artistic technique. During the 1950's he would take natural and common materials such as leaves and grass and, soaking them in ink, imprint them onto paper. By the same means he would transfer their images onto lithographic stones. Cutting up these imprints, he also was able to create collages having figurative elements that he would further emphasize by outlining their forms with crayon or ink.

The direct imprints became a sort of catalog of textures from which Dubuffet could select those appropriate to his theme. This idea was expanded when Dubuffet made his *Phenomena* series of lithographs: 234 different black-and-white prints made from transferred imprints and some other direct methods (heated resin, mixtures of water and turpentine). From this library of textural images Dubuffet also created color prints by superimposing several of the black-and-white plates in as many colors. These color lithographs were also part of the *Phenomena* series and were to act as the artist's palette for collages. *Carrot Nose* is one of the prints that was produced from this palette. The humorous figure was developed from a collage of cutout *Phenomena* sheets, each of which had a number that indicated to the printer the stones and colors he was to use. [See color plate on cover.]

Pierre Alechinsky   Belgian, born 1927
The Moon. (1969), Georges Visat, Paris.
Lithograph and aquatint, 21-5/16 x 29⅞″.

By combining aquatint and lithography in this print, Pierre Alechinsky has created an effect similar to that of some of his paintings in which a central painted panel containing the major subject is surrounded by a border of separately executed drawings on paper. In these compositions the borders form a decorative frame for the main panel as well as an environment of simultaneous happenings. The small vignettes that make up the border of this print are like random frames from an old film or comic strip. Where recognizable elements appear in the midst of meanders and other calligraphic forms, they tend to extend the pictorial cliché, a moon shining on the sea, that is depicted in the center.

The combination of two media in one print may be compared to pages of illustrated books in which photographs or special printing techniques are used for the illustrations and a different press and often different paper are used for the typography. In Alechinsky's print the texture and color of the essentially blue-black ink have quite a different appearance in each area. The harmony of dissimilar surfaces enhances the total image.

Pierre Alechinsky was a member of the COBRA group when it was formed in 1948 of artists from Copenhagen, Brussels, and Amsterdam. The artists and writers of the group were interested in automatism, the gestural process of making art, and the folk subjects of their countries. Alechinsky was particularly influenced by his countryman James Ensor, in whose works Alechinsky found many of his mischievous and somewhat satanic characters.

Friedensreich Hundertwasser
(Friedrich Stowasser)   Austrian, born 1928
Good Morning City, Bleeding Town. 1970, Galerie
Leonhart, Munich.
Color serigraph, embossed, 30⅛ x 19½".

The Austrian version of art nouveau during the early
1900's was named after the Viennese secession
movement. In the hands of its best known painter,
Gustav Klimt, complex geometric and spiral patterns
overwhelmed the subject matter. Friedensreich
Hundertwasser, who altered his real name, Friedrich Stowasser, in order to have a more symbolic
connotation, has taken Klimt's convoluted decorative elements and made of them an imaginary and
sometimes frightening environment. Although he
also uses gold, as did Klimt, as well as more recently
developed metallic materials, his colors are harsh
reds, yellows, and greens rather than the muted
tones of art nouveau.

   This embossed silkscreen is based on a painting of
1952 entitled *Bleeding Houses* and is Hundertwasser's 686th work. Like all his prints, it is a variation
on earlier work in which the customary processes
and idiosyncracies of printmaking change the focus
of the image. This print, for example, carries the
trademarks of all those companies and persons involved in its production. There is also a guide anno-
tating the eighteen colors used. Perhaps the most
fascinating aspect of this print is the size of the edition (ten thousand) and the computer-like method
of its printing. There are fifty variations in the placement of colors in the edition. The block of letters in
the lower left gives the formula for the combinations.
[See color plate, page 11.]

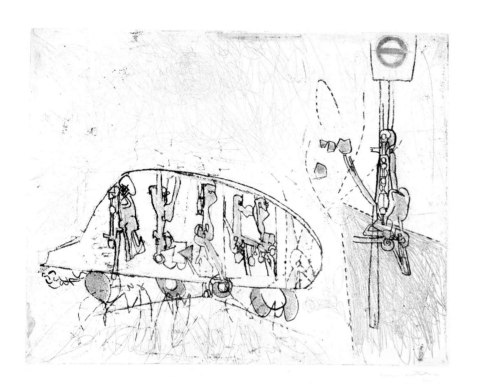

Matta (Sebastian Antonio Matta Echaurren)
Chilean, born 1912
The Bus from *Scènes Familiers.* (1962), Le Point
Cardinal, Paris.
Color etching, 12⅞ x 17".
Private collection.

In 1944 Matta executed his first figurative work, a
portrait of André Breton, the poet and leader of the
surrealist movement, to which Matta belonged. In
this painting Matta developed a unique sort of an-
thropomorph, which began to populate his other
compositions. The forms of these beings often depended on their function (for example, embracing,
they would appear all arms), and they frequently incorporated bits of machinery in their bizarre anat-
omies. This print of *The Bus* is from a portfolio devoted to scenes in Paris. It shows these creatures
being bounced along, seeming to defy gravity, in the
capsule-like confines of the autobus. The anthro-
pomorphic object at the right combines a sign post
(holding the international sign for "Do not enter")
with a moving form that may or may not be a police-
man.

Matta uses for his etchings a technique known as
soft ground. After placing a varnish on his copper
plate which remains relatively soft, he covers it with
thin paper and draws his composition. The varnish
is pushed away where the pencil or other pointed
instrument impresses the paper, and the lines that
result after etching and printing resemble those
made by very soft pencil, crayon, or ball-point pen.

Joan Miró   Spanish, born 1893
Stars and Smoke. 1968, Aimé Maeght, Paris.
Color etching and aquatint, 29⅞ x 22⅛".
Collection Mr. and Mrs. Robert Dain, New York.

This is one of the more than fifty etchings Joan Miró
made immediately before his seventy-fifth birthday.
It incorporates several of the formal elements he introduced into his work many decades earlier during
his association with the surrealists. The title *Stars
and Smoke* describes this etching completely. Liquid
washes form the smoky passages that swirl around
the crusty star-disks. Rasping linear jottings are
magical messages in a code devised by the artist.
This abstract, placeless composition is typical of the
abandoned gaiety of Miró's inventively modern spirit.
    In this print the artist has explored the conjunc-
tions of brightly colored geometric forms with less
controllable washes. The successful juxtaposition
of these elements, particularly of their plastic values,
came about through the use of a new technique. Using a material consisting of carborundum particles
suspended in a synthetic resin, Miró was able to
apply directly to the plate textures equivalent to
aquatint and etching. Miró wrote, "I can express my-
self without a single hindrance, at a single burst of
spirit, without being paralyzed nor slowed down by
an outmoded technique that might risk distorting the
free expression, purity and freshness of the final result." Spontaneity and rhythm were basic factors in
the artistic developments occurring in the decade
after World War II. Miró displays in his work the roots
from which some of these developments grew.

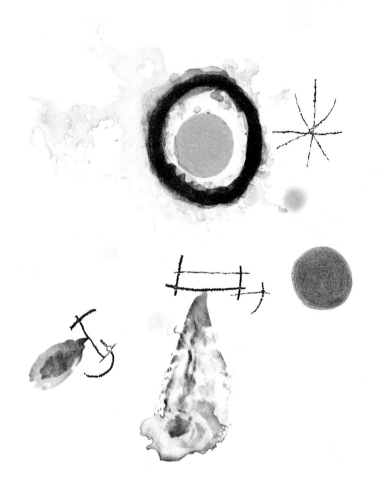

Hans Hartung   French, born Germany 1904
Brown Composition. (1965), Galerie Im Erker,
St. Gallen.
Color lithograph, 17 x 23½".

As early as 1922 Hans Hartung began to subdue figurative elements in his watercolors, emphasizing the surrounding forms, so that his work became abstract in character. Preferring to work in a more expressionist mode, he rejected the cubists and even Kandinsky. Hartung pursued his form of abstract art devotedly and without any appreciable acceptance until after World War II, when the disoriented, war-torn world seemed more receptive to a freer sort of expression than the geometrical abstraction so popular in the 1930's.

Hartung's line, moving across a nebulous mass, has a time and emotional value that creates a sense of impending revelation. It reflects his youthful interest in lightning, thunder, and other sudden, intangible elements that instilled in him a sensitivity to movement, time, distance, and rhythm.

Born in Germany, Hartung became a French citizen in 1946, the same year he began to make lithographs. His lithographs of the 1960's became increasingly simple, generally consisting of a few deft crayon lines caught together by diagonals or in feathered clusters. In this print he has reversed the positive and negative elements so that the flat-edged strokes appear scraped into a solid ground. While most of his prints are straight-bordered compositions worked well within the limits of the lithographic stone, this is one of the few prints in which Hartung incorporated the natural, irregular outline of the stone in his composition.

Pierre Soulages   French, born 1919
Composition. (1964), Lacourière, Paris.
Etching, 23 x 16¾".

There is a primal relationship between the broad,
dark drama of the paintings and prints of Pierre
Soulages and the heavy Romanesque architecture
that dominates the area of France where he grew up.
The thick, black strokes made with a wide scraper,
even though they convey the physical gesture of their
facture, are sturdy architectural members of each
composition. Black has been the mainstay of Soulages's work from the time he was a child and preferred to draw the leafless winter trees. His first postwar works were closer to linear calligraphy than the
bold emblems he began to compose in the mid-
1950's. At whatever period, however, black has been
dominant and in this etching it surrounds and illum-
inates a window of color.

Soulages's etching is printed from a copper plate
that has been very deeply bitten with acid. The irregular edges of the etched portion of the composition
are the limits of the plate after the mordant has eaten
completely through the metal. The plate itself remains as a provocative relic. Its contours and irregular surface translate themselves, through printing,
into a tactile sign that finds its specific form in its
imposition on white paper.

Soulages thinks of his work in poetic rather than
gestural terms. He concentrates his creative force
on evolving one complete statement that, like a perfect stanza in poetry or a single calligraphic sign, is
totally destroyed by the change of even one element.
Soulages's compositions have the hermetic magnet-
ism of meditative objects. [See color plate, page 12.]

Antoni Tàpies   Spanish, born 1923
Two Blacks and Cardboard. (1972), Aimé Maeght,
Paris.
Color embossed lithograph, 14¼ x 16-13/16".

Antoni Tàpies is one of the European artists who
turned to a more gestural art after some years of surrealist painting. A native of Catalonia, that magic
area of Spain in which Picasso developed and where
its most famous resident artist, Joan Miró, still works,
Tàpies had quite a large burden of influences to as-
similate. He found the used materials of his environment of particular interest: dented and scratched
doors, defaced land, graffiti, scraps of cast-off
goods. He translated these forms into paintings that
retained the tactile qualities of these corruptions.

In print, through collage and embossing, Tàpies is
able to convey some of the same tactility. This lithograph has been embossed to produce the appearance of a piece of old corrugated cardboard. The
shape is not literal, and although it has implicit references to reality, it is formed solely by imagination.
Tàpies takes the disregarded part of our surround-
ings and placing an element of it on a white sheet of
paper realigns and refocuses our sensitivities.

Willem de Kooning
American, born the Netherlands 1904
Minnie Mouse. 1971, Hollanders Workshop, Inc.,
New York.
Lithograph, 27½ x 21".

The American abstract expressionist artists were not at first concerned with finding a large audience for their images through the print media. Although Jackson Pollock grasped at the idea of automatic drawing during his few sessions at Hayter's New York Atelier 17, he sought a new form of painting rather than a devotion to printmaking. Willem de Kooning, well after he was established as one of the foremost artists of the New York school of action painting, made two lithographs in 1960. This dizzying image of *Minnie Mouse* is one of more than twenty lithographs he executed a decade later.

Because gesture is such an important part of de Kooning's style, the known limitations of the stones and presses of lithography undoubtedly made him approach the medium with some trepidation. At the beginning he worked exclusively with transfer paper drawings. By the time this print was done, he had found his individual manner of working directly on the stone. The active brush strokes, dazzling like a prize fighter's footwork, play all over the composition, revealing and distorting de Koonig's comic version of his familiar image of woman. The Walt Disney cartoon character has her traditional attributes: oversized high-heeled shoes and a hair ribbon. These recognizable signs are solidly enmeshed in the frenzy of swirling areas of washes that are the emotive element of the composition. An aura of excitement and the expectation of some truly hilarious action are conveyed by the lines that emerge from this lovely chaos of unfettered expression.

Sam Francis   American, born 1923
Untitled. (1969), Tamarind Lithography Workshop,
Los Angeles.
Color lithograph, 20 x 30".
The Museum of Modern Art, New York (promised
gift of Kleiner, Bell and Company).

In 1959 Sam Francis, the American abstract expressionist painter who has spent most of his career in Europe and Japan, painted a mural in New York. While there he began to make lithographs, and although his first efforts remained uncompleted until 1968, Francis was the first major artist of his generation to utilize the medium with the direct facture of the action painter. His work has an affinity with the Japanese *haboku,* or "flung ink," style of drawing. His first published lithographs were free and colorful, drippings swirling across generous areas of white paper. The paper was a wall, an environment upon which the colors found their form in dazzling contrast.

This print was executed at the Tamarind Lithography Workshop in Los Angeles, California, where Francis has often been the guest artist. (This workshop was created to develop master lithographic printers and introduce professional practicing painters and sculptors to the medium.) In order to make a color lithograph the artist works only with black. In this case using brush and tusche, Francis created his abstract composition directly on the number of stones he needed (one for printing each color) without knowing how the images would look superimposed. The printer then carried out the arduous work of printing all the stones together, occasionally reversing one or two of the stones in direction, and making many color proofs in order to determine a sequence for the final printing. This process necessitated a close collaboration between artist and printer, as only during proofing was the artist able to establish his final composition. The liquid strokes and splashes, their subtle washes preserved with great care by the printer, retain the verve and spontaneity of Francis's personal gesture.

Ellsworth Kelly   American, born 1923
Variant II, Yellow. (1965), Aimé Maeght, Paris.
Color lithograph, 23¼ x 15-7/16″.

This monochromatic composition by the American
painter and sculptor Ellsworth Kelly is part of a series
of lithographs he executed in France in 1964. He had
envisioned a group of prints that would be a compil-
ation of his ideas of color relationships based on
sixty-four combinations of color, using identical compositions. Instead, the series was limited to twenty-
seven prints of eleven different compositions. As
many as seven variations in color were accom-
plished for two of the compositions, but several were
unique images and opposed the paper's white field
with a single bold form in one color. The series taken
altogether is an abridged dictionary of Kelly's form
and color preferences.

Like his American contemporary Sam Francis,
Kelly spent the early years of his artistic career in
Paris. Before his return to the United States in 1954,
he had made automatic drawings and worked with
the chance collages that were to lead to the development of his bold style based on the integrity of color.
Kelly's use of cut paper collage relates indirectly to
the work of Henri Matisse and Jean Arp. However,
Kelly's work is essentially about color itself; the
shapes in which he confines his color are adjusted
according to the vibrancy and weight dictated by the
chosen color or colors. In this print the white paper
is not a background for the double curve of yellow,
but rather the field into which it spreads and finds
form.

Helen Frankenthaler American, born 1928
Nepenthe. 1972, John Berggruen, San Francisco.
Color etching and aquatint, 15¾ x 24¼".

The New York environment during the late 1940's offered incredible possibilities to the young art student who wanted to succeed. For Helen Frankenthaler all the opportunities—the right teachers and acquaintances—allowed her to make the sensitive and intelligent observations that led to her development as an important member of the second generation of New York abstract expressionists. Her awareness of Kandinsky's work, which she saw displayed in depth at the Guggenheim Museum, led her toward abstraction. Jackson Pollock's method of dripping paint on a canvas laid on the floor led her to work that way, off the easel. However, Frankenthaler developed her own method and style: the staining of raw canvas with diluted color spilled onto the canvas and allowed to soak into it.

Frankenthaler made her first lithographs in 1960 at the same studio outside New York City where Jasper Johns and Robert Rauschenberg also began. She learned etching methods there in 1969. This print was made in California and shows the character of her stain method in the pale veil of aquatint that forms the central subject. As the name implies, aquatint is meant to look like a watercolor or ink wash. The artist accomplishes the effect by sprinkling powdered resin on the copper or zinc plate, heating the plate, which melts and fixes the bits of resin, then putting the plate into an acid bath. The acid will only eat away the plate where it remains exposed between the hardened granules. The etched strokes of bright color create a spatial activity over which spreads the aquatinted cloud of *Nepenthe,* the drug of oblivion. [See color plate, page 13.]

Barnett Newman   American, 1905–1970
Untitled. 1969, Universal Limited Art Editions,
West Islip.
Etching and aquatint, 14-13/16 x 23⅜".
Collection S. I. Newhouse, Jr., New York.

An apparently simple compositional division made
by vertical lines of varying widths became a profound and emotionally charged expression in the
hands of the American painter Barnett Newman. A
vocal and brilliant spokesman for the New York
school of action painters, he developed a style in
which the active elements typical of their work became concentrated and more intense. This charged
form he called a "zip," the vertical form that slashed
through fields of flat, inert color. Toward the end of
his life the plastic handling of the zips became increasingly austere until, in this print, the edges of the
black strips have a uniformity that evokes the monumental and peaceful.

   This etching was one of two compositions Newman completed shortly before his death. He had
been asked to make a memorial print for Martin
Luther King, and before executing it he experimented
with the etching techniques. This stark image, its in-
tensely black, aquatinted, vertical stripe subjected to
the unequal division of a white field cut into by narrow etched lines, is probably the basis for the totally
black memorial aquatint that remained unprinted at
Newman's death.

Robert Rauschenberg   American, born 1925
Lawn. (1965), Universal Limited Art Editions,
West Islip.
Color lithograph, 31½ x 23¾".

Robert Rauschenberg has written about his prints,
"My lithography is the realization and execution of
the fact that anything that creates an image on stone
is potential material. The image that is made by a
printer's mat, a metal plate, a wet glass or a leaf
plastically incorporated into a composition and applied to a stone, stops functioning literally within its
previous limitations. They are an artistic recording of
an action as realistic and poetic as a brush stroke."

   This course of creative action is well shown in
Rauschenberg's twenty-eighth lithograph *Lawn.* He
has taken an old commercial lithographic stone already carrying the image of graph paper on it and
used it as the unifying element for the freely executed
black overprinting. The green graph is a verdant environment for Rauschenberg's brush strokes, imprints, and frottages. He made the photographic passages by inking the printer's mats (molded paper that
carries in relief the type and photographs for printing
newspapers) and imprinting them on the stone. At
the left are images he made by rubbing newspaper
and magazine illustration onto the stone (President
John F. Kennedy is shown in the upper left). Lithographic crayon and tusche are used to trap the dis-
parate images and vivify the composition. Rauschenberg's combination of gestural marks and recognizable, mechanically made images from commercial
sources has been considered the transitional style
that led from abstract expressionism to pop art.

Jasper Johns American, born 1930
Two Maps II. 1966, Universal Limited Art Editions,
West Islip.
Lithograph, 25-9/16 x 20¾".

These two almost identical maps of the United States
of America form a single composition that has a
compelling drama far beyond the subject matter. Indeed, for Jasper Johns, the map of his native land is
a study in the arrangement of a surface, the magical
derivation of three forms from the conjunction of two.
The contrived boundaries of the states, all of which
have been greatly distorted by the artist, still provide recognition, since the pattern is, for an American, instilled in the mind as one of the earliest bits
of abstract knowledge. Johns himself speaks of
places in the world as being unknown to him unless
he has visited them. Raised in an isolated area,
where he was taught by people who had traveled
little or not at all, Johns was not equipped with ideas
of relative distance and placement that allowed him
to build an image of geographical reality other than
that he had learned as an abstract symbol.

Johns's lithographs are often technical master-
pieces. The sensitive use of a printing medium is
particularly evident in black-and-white prints. Johns's
respect for the black-and-white lithographs of Odilon
Redon, the nineteenth-century symbolist, has been
an important part of his inspiration. When he began
making prints at Universal Limited Art Editions in
1960, he became conscious of the subtle values of
black attainable in lithography. In *Two Maps II* Johns
has created an ordered mass of shaped puddles of
liquid which has been printed in black on a thin sheet
of white Japan paper, pasted to a larger sheet of
black. The delicate filaments that form the washes
are given considerable clarity by being printed on
the fine texture of the Japan paper.

Frank Stella   American, born 1936
Quathlamba II. 1968, Gemini G.E.L., Los Angeles.
Color lithograph, 11-1/16 x 25⅞".
Collection David Whitney, New York.

The names Frank Stella applied to his *Notched V* series of paintings in 1964—1965 often were those of British clipper ships. This print *Quathlamba II* is one of a series of eight lithographs Stella made at Gemini G.E.L. in Los Angeles after the *Notched V* paintings. The three joined wedges are of different colors, and vibrate from the activity of the bands that reiterate their shapes. The insistent lateral movement set up by the angularized snaking form is slowed down by the buttressing action of the individual V's. The bands themselves are slightly irregular, creating hesitating rhythms in the uncolored spaces between them. Stella's flat patterned compositions show the influence of Jasper Johns's flag paintings. A comparison of *Quathlamba II* with Johns's *Two Maps II* will show that negative delineation, that is, allowing the positive forms to create their own definitive borders, is another formal element shared by the two artists.

Part of the importance of Stella's work is his contribution to the development of the shaped canvas in the 1960's. The *Notched V* paintings derived a great part of their focus from their edges. In the lithographs one must see the printed image as on a wall of white. However, the contiguousness of the white in the lithographs, wherein the areas between the bands are on the same plane as the background, creates a different dimension to Stella's prints. The ink, too, is a translation from the metallic powder in polymer used for the paintings to a slick, reflecting ink in metal-like tones.

Eduardo Paolozzi   British, born 1924
Conjectures to Identity. (1964), Institute of Contemporary Art, London.
Color serigraph, 29-11/16 x 19-7/16".
The Museum of Modern Art, New York
(Joseph G. Mayer Foundation Fund).

One of the foremost influences in the work of the British sculptor Eduardo Paolozzi appears to be the collages of the surrealist Max Ernst. Ernst combined parts of Victorian woodengravings to present fantastic narratives worthy of Freudian dream analysis. For his prints Paolozzi chooses his imagery from a different source: illustrations from scientific and popular journals and manuals, interspersed with color patterns. He provokes a sort of mechanical scanning reaction to his seemingly randomly chosen and uniquely arranged imagery. The saturation of our visual environment with manufactured images and data is reflected in such screenprints as *Conjectures to Identity*. Paolozzi has chosen parts of illustrations of machinery and machine parts, a photograph not contemporaneous with the print, patterns of checks and lines, all partitioned by uneven areas of color. The manner of placement recalls the commercial artist's "paste-up" of diverse advertising material. This print represents a microcosm of man's continual experience of being bombarded with an unassimilable quantity of visual facts and abstract ideas.

This work has been printed from screens photographically processed after a collage. The British prefer to use the term screenprinting instead of silkscreen or serigraph since they generally use a synthetic material instead of silk for their screens. In the photographic method the stencil that prevents ink from going through the screen is made by means of exposing to light a light-sensitive gelatin covering with a photographic transparency over it. The gelatin is hardened only where the light hits it, and the remainder is washed away, reopening the portions of the screen where the image is for the passage of ink. Five screens (one for each color) have been used for this print.

Helebore: for Georg Trakl.

Ronald B. Kitaj   American, born 1932
Hellebore: for George Trakl from *Mahler Becomes Politics, Beisbol.* (1965), Marlborough Fine Arts, London.
Color serigraph, 28 x 19-3/16".

Like Paolozzi's print, this work by R. B. Kitaj is a screenprint made from a collage. Kitaj is an American who has created most of his prints in London, where he and Paolozzi are friends. Paolozzi, however, uses images in his works predominantly as visual statements, while Kitaj is deeply involved in a contemporary iconography incorporating literary and historical elements. The visual enjoyment of this print, *Hellebore: for George Trakl,* is extended by some understanding of the apparently unrelated images of which it is composed.

In 1964 Kitaj began work on a group of prints entitled *Mahler Becomes Politics, Beisbol* that were based loosely on the poetry of Jonathan Williams inspired by Gustav Mahler's symphonies. Several of the screenprints include Williams's poems as well as visual references to the Viennese composer's period (*i.e.,* decorative designs of the early 1900's). The title of this print refers to the Austrian poet, George Trakl, Mahler's contemporary, whose work Kitaj has admired since his own studies in Vienna in 1951. In fact, Viennese-grown thought has been an important influence in Kitaj's iconography, derived in good part from the ideas of the philosopher Ludwig Wittgenstein. Kitaj has created collage compositions as visualizations of Wittgenstein's theories on the arrangement of information. The artist also found Wittgenstein's comment on Trakl's poetry ("I don't understand it, but its tone delights me") a suitable musical reference for the inclusion of Trakl in a work on Mahler.

Paul Wunderlich   German, born 1927
Zebra Blouse. 1969, Desjobert, Paris.
Color lithograph, 25¾ x 19-13/16".

Among the objects with which the German lithographer and painter Paul Wunderlich surrounds himself in the slightly decadent setting of his apartment in Hamburg is a zebra-skin carpet. When Wunderlich introduces the carpet into his prints, the undulating stripes of the skin evoke memories of the decorative styles of the early 1900's. He equates the awkward proportions of the furnishings of that period with attenuated female creatures who emerge from the haze of his compositions as from a dream. In the lithograph *Zebra Blouse* these decorative and surreal manifestations are found in a smoky mauve interior, which seems to exude a sense of mystery and sexual provocation.

Wunderlich's Germanic fantasy is served particularly well by the quality of his lithographic technique. His knowledge of lithography actually increases the range of his art although he admits "too much technical brilliance is not necessarily a good thing. Technically I am good; few are as good, but things should not come too easily." The five colors of this print, violet, ochre, blue, turquoise, and black, model the forms as much as the drawing does, and mix together to add subtle variation to the pervasive mauve tonality. Wunderlich presents one attitude about reality that most often manifests itself in an examination of woman. The sense of the socially or emotionally abnormal so apparent in these studies is one of the links he maintains with the satirists such as Grosz and the symbolists such as Klinger and the early Kubin.

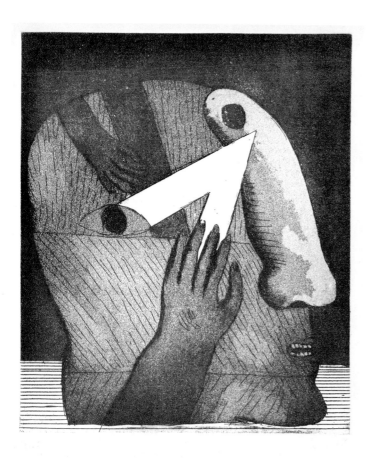

Horst Antes   German, born 1936
Head with Angle. (1966).
Etching, 9⅝ x 8-1/16".

In the early 1960's Horst Antes devised a figure with human characteristics that, with only superficial transformations, was to populate all his paintings and prints. Its head was the helmet-skull of Etruscan sculpture with one or two eyes placed on one side in the manner of Picasso's work after 1938. This imposing object rested upon a minimal torso and mammoth legs. Throughout Antes's work this figure, and particularly its head, has been subjected to decoration and mutilation. The actions of the figure take place in stagelike settings containing confusing clues as to depth and direction. The figure itself is nearly flat and confined to a narrow track parallel to the picture plane.

Like many other artists who were youngsters during World War II, Antes seems to be concerned with man's inability to control the results of his own actions. For this purpose he has created this quasirobot to be his "everyman." The etched head of 1966, somewhat vicious with its small mouth full of sharp teeth, is compartmentalized by horizontal lines and disturbed by the intrusion of a white angle held up against it by an alien hand. The appearance of a second descending hand recalls the Byzantine representation of God's hand offering the laws to Moses. Antes has previously given his figure the stigmata of Christ, and there are other instances in which he has taken elements from Italian Byzantine and Renaissance art to impart a message about contemporary man.

David Hockney   British, born 1937
Home from *Six Fairy Tales from the Brothers Grimm.*
1969, Petersburg Press, London.
Etching, 17-5/16 x 12-5/16".
The Museum of Modern Art, New York
(Monroe Wheeler Fund).

In 1961 David Hockney began his first series of etchings, an autobiographical parody of William Hogarth's *A Rake's Progress.* In Hockney's version, for example, the episode in which the rake receives his inheritance is transformed into a scene of an artist bartering with a collector over the sale of an etching. This manner of relating a classical episode to the reality of the present appears again in some of the etchings Hockney made to illustrate *Six Fairy Tales from the Brothers Grimm.* In the simple line etching *Home,* which appears at the beginning of the tale "The Boy who Left Home to Learn Fear," there is no sense of the historical period of the tale nor the element of fantasy generally found in such illustrations. Instead Hockney shows the bright, airy, comfortable interior of a contemporary British home in the country. The furnishings are those sorts of nondescript objects that embody a personal remembrance of home.

This print is a typical line etching: After covering the copper or zinc plate with a varnish that dries to a hard surface (called hard ground), the artist scratches his drawing into it with a stylus; the places where the drawing occurs, having exposed the plate, are bitten into when the plate is put into an acid bath. The printed image is made by rubbing ink into the etched lines and running the inked plate and paper through a press.

Hockney's dry line creates a detached, unemotional sense to his compositions. Light has no source, but bathes the entire scene indiscriminately. There is an utter stillness in *Home* that, as the Grimm's story unfolds, becomes easily reinterpreted, changing from an atmosphere of security to an abandoned place of loneliness.

Richard Hamilton   British, born 1922
The Solomon R. Guggenheim. (August, 1965),
Editions Alecto, London.
Color serigraph, 22 x 22".
Private collection.

The Solomon R. Guggenheim Museum in New York, designed by Frank Lloyd Wright and completed in 1959, had a unique shape that offered considerable ground for controversy. It was one of the few serious pieces of creative architecture after World War II that became a popular image. During his first visit to America in 1963 the British artist Richard Hamilton saw this modern landmark. A year later he became intrigued by the Greek temples that were then appearing in Roy Lichtenstein's paintings, and decided to base a new work on a modern building. Previously he had chosen the stylizations of commercial advertising for his imagery. Now he was interested in the type of architectural visualization that altered the appearance of a structure by exaggerating certain elements (*i.e.*, in the case of institutional buildings, for monumental effect).

Hamilton found the sort of rendering he was seeking in a postcard of the Guggenheim Museum sent to him by the Museum's Curator, Lawrence Alloway, a friend and former collaborator. Predisposed toward the banal, the building's notorious spiral structure perhaps reminded him of the construction of brassieres so often represented in advertising. In this screenprint the false perspective emphasizes the bulging upper stories while the peach-pink color, rendered in the slick manner of cheap commercial reproduction, may allude to either women's undergarments or certain types of inexpensive plastic. Both this print and the drawings made after the postcard preceded a series of fiberglass reliefs painted in ways that deliberately confused the already distorted form.

Jim Dine American, born 1935
The World for Anne Waldman. 1972, Petersburg
Press, London.
Color lithograph, serigraph, woodblock, collage, and
pencil, 30-9/16 x 39¾".

In the Lower East Side of New York City at a church
built on the Bowerie, the farm of the seventeenth-
century Dutchman Peter Stuyvesant, a poet's workshop is run by the young poetess Anne Waldman.
Anne Waldman became the coordinator of a poetry
magazine, *The World,* in which she published poems
from the workshop as well as her own. The American
artist Jim Dine, whose style is usually associated
with pop art, is also a poet, and his admiration for
Anne Waldman is given form in this print. The words
are in the style of her poetry, in which only the names
of places or objects form a picture of an idea. In the
text on the print the world (the place as well as the
magazine) consists of the names of cities, states,
and a restaurant. Seed catalogue reproductions of
vegetables (the world is a turnip?), typographical
elements, thin lines (boundaries on a map?), and a
series of eleven hearts (one in colors of the rainbow,
a favorite motif of Dine) form several structural patterns that lead to varied readings of the words that
accompany them.

Technically the most complex print in this selection, elements are put together that Dine has used
elsewhere in watercolors and collages. Ten of the
hearts are lithographic, two printed flatly and the
others very freely handled with washes. The rainbow
heart and the collages of vegetables are screen-
printed. The typographical alphabet is printed from
woodblock letters. The individual words are written
by hand. This print has been handled at least thirty-
two times: eleven passages through the lithography
press, five times under the screenprinting frame,
three gluings of collage, twelve individual block-
printings, and one session of handwriting. [See color
plate, page 14.]

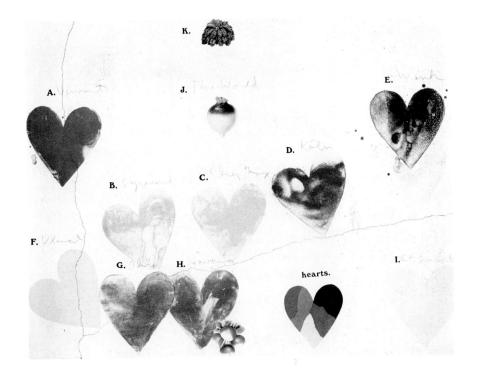

Roy Lichtenstein   American, born 1923
Sweet Dreams, Baby! from *11 Pop Artists.* (1965),
Original Editions, New York.
Color serigraph, 35¾ x 25-9/16".
Private Collection.

Comic strips became sources of subject matter for several artists during the early 1960's. The economy of line and color in popular newspaper cartoons appealed to Roy Lichtenstein, who was searching for a ready-made subject that would allow him to concentrate on balancing formal elements and achieving a high degree of unity in his compositions. He isolated one frame from a strip, abstracting its generally plaintive or violent messages by taking it out of context. He then subtly reorganized the standard elements of the composition by redrawing the heavy black lines and altering the areas of dots (in the preparation of cartoons for printing shadows and areas of color spaces in the original line drawings are filled with preprinted sheets of dots known in the commercial art trade as Ben Day Dots).

Sweet Dreams, Baby! is typical of Lichtenstein's interpretation of cartoon elements, the dots presenting an insistent pattern that transforms eyes, hair, and words into abstract images. The silkscreen technique is an ideal means of rendering the sharp edges and flat colors of the lines and dots. No subtle changes in intensity occur to diminish the electrifying effect of Lichtenstein's bold forms. [See color plate, page 15.]

Andy Warhol   American, born 1930
Marilyn. (1967), Leo Castelli, New York.
Color serigraph, 36 x 36″.
Collection David Whitney, New York.

Formerly one of the most prominent commercial
artists in New York City, Andy Warhol turned to the
creation of paintings and prints by means of the
silkscreen in 1962. The same image of the American
screen star Marilyn Monroe was used consistently by
Warhol for five years. This high contrast photoimage,
broken into the dots of halftone reproduction, appeared as many as fifty times in one work, the
Marilyn Diptych. The lips were isolated and looked
like 168 butterflies in another work.

In this example from a portfolio of ten Marilyns
published in 1967 Warhol has isolated elements of
the portrait and printed them in flat colors under the
photographed image. The lipstick, eyeshadow, hair,
and collar are emphasized by the use of disruptive,
stinging poster colors that heighten the sense of the
artificiality of the movie queen's tragic life. In fact
there are two portraits: the photograph, a distortion
of what is considered real, and the mask, the truth.

Warhol's attitude toward art is found in the process
he applies to its manufacture. He takes the familiar
images of newspaper reportage and advertising pro-
motion and translates them by means of the distor-
tions of his medium—silkscreen—into art. Although
his subjects appear to be photographs of tragedy
(automobile crashes, Jacqueline Kennedy mourn-
ing her husband) and prosaic advertising designs
(soup cans, Brillo boxes, wallpaper), the medium
dominates each image.

Victor Vasarely French, born Hungary 1908
Permutation #1. (1968), Denise René, Paris.
Color serigraph, 23⅝ x 23⅝".

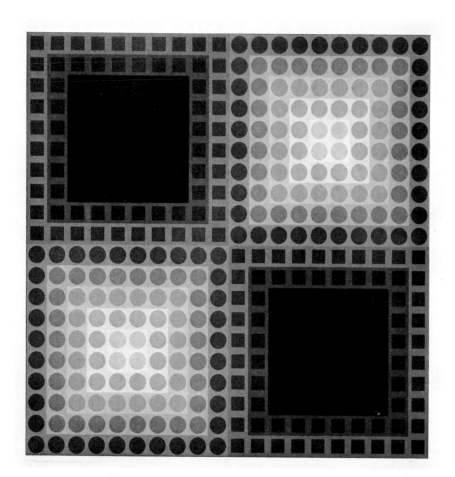

Among the prints in which Victor Vasarely utilizes his idea of plastic unity—the integration and inseparability of form and color—is this silkscreen from the album *Permutations.* The artist has created an alphabet of binary units consisting of squares containing another form (square, circle, oval, and so on) that, put together in rows, form his compositions. This print has four parts, each containing a serial arrangement of a hundred units which combine colors (in this case shades of red and blue) to provide the contrasts necessary to stimulate a visual sense of spatial movement. An opposition of movement is set up by increasingly darker and lighter shades within the four modules. The square-upon-square units actually resolve into four units of brown on black but continue to give the illusion of red and blue in the distant darkness.

Vasarely, formerly a commercial artist whose teacher was a student of the Bauhaus, turned from his profession to creating a type of art that would be available and intelligible to the masses. Since Vasarely felt that art that required interpretation based on experience would not be mass art, he chose to use forms that would provide only visual sensations. He has advocated the return of art to its role as an integral part of life and has conceived of his images as infinitely multipliable in prints, sculptures, games, and architectural environments. Since his imagery is modular and serial, it has the capacity for almost limitless variation. [See color plate, page 16.]

Jesus Rafael Soto   Venezuelan, born 1923
Plate 8 from *Caroni.* (1971), Denise René—Hans
Mayer, Dusseldorf.
Color serigraph, 22-9/16 x 15-5/16".

One of the pioneers in the creation of kinetic struc-
tures during the 1950's was Jesus Rafael Soto.
These works evolved from his study of relationships
of color and form and the influences of the paintings
of Mondrian. His kinetic works utilize repetitive motifs
that set up vibrations which alter their relationships.
In many compositions he opposes a fixed field of
parallel narrow lines with thin wires whose movements, mechanical or natural, disturb the visual
constancy of the linear field. Generally, the most successful visual disturbances, which Soto prefers to be
indeterminate, are based on three-dimensional elements. When the agitating structure is placed in an
area slightly removed from the stable element, the
movement of either the spectator or the free structure
contributes to the initiation of vibrating sensations.

This silkscreen is a two-dimensional translation of
a group of works in which solid-colored squares
protrude from the linear plane. In the print no element is outside the picture plane to kinetically disturb
the pattern, yet, as the eye passes over the composition and encounters the colored squares, certain
slight muscular compensations occur in the eye that
induce a sense of vibration between the lines and
squares.

Josef Albers   American, born Germany 1888
White Line Square IV. 1966, Gemini G.E.L.,
Los Angeles.
Color lithograph, 15¾ x 15¾".

After 1949 Josef Albers devoted most of his creative effort to a concept he has called *Homage to the Square.* By means of a series of superimposed squares, each varying in color or tonality based on his prolonged practical experience of the effects of color, Albers has explored in this self-imposed, confined structure the mysteries of both color and shape. The square forms are given spatial distinction by the illusion of changes of tone at the outer and inner perimeters of each band. The white, uninked line in this work adds another dimensional element to the densely printed lithograph.

This print is one of a series of sixteen on the theme *White Line Square,* the first set of lithographs printed by Gemini G.E.L. in Los Angeles. The success of the image is dependent upon a totally unmarred and unreflecting printed surface and the precise registration of the three color plates in order to give perfect definition to the exposed white line. Nevertheless, the result is not identical to what might be made by machine alone, but only shares with machine-made works the appearance of mathematical exactness.

A student and teacher at the Bauhaus for thirteen years, Albers reflects in his theories his concern with visual growth in a technological society. He prefers to use commercially prepared paints and inks and drafting tools, and has created prints by means of computer-activated machinery. His theories of color have been set forth in his book *Interaction of Color.*

Sol LeWitt   American, born 1928
Untitled. (1971), Parasol Press, New York.
Etching, comp. 2-11/16 x 11-11/16".

The American artist Sol LeWitt shares with many of
his contemporaries the idea that object-making is
only an incidental episode in the making of art. This
etching is, to him, a byproduct of the actual funda-
mental process of art, the concept or idea. The sim-
plicity of the system of this particular concept could
well allow others to extend it into two-dimensional
space, and similar systems have been realized in
walldrawings by persons instructed by LeWitt. This
etching follows the system of straight lines in four
directions. It is less pure than the concept since the
vagaries of the medium have caused the wavering
lines, specks of ink, and irregular surface to become
as important as the idea they imperfectly convey.

LeWitt has written some sentences that illuminate
his attitude: "Once the idea of the piece is established in the artist's mind and the final form is decided, the process is carried out blindly. There are
many side effects that the artist cannot imagine. . . ."
"The process is mechanical and should not be
tampered with. It should run its course." The visual
results of LeWitt's concepts have the beauty of simple mathematics in which an abstract idea has
infinite possibilities.

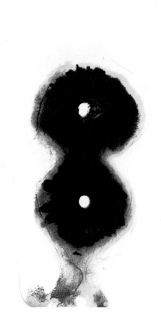

Otto Piene   German, born 1928
Untitled from *Rose Oder Stern*. 1965, Editions
Rottloff, Karlsruhe.
Color serigraph, 17¼ x 11⅝".
The Museum of Modern Art, New York (Joseph M.
Edinburg Fund).

The postwar use of artificial light as an artistic medium often depended on the parallel development of
environmental art. The effectiveness of light art
generally required a setting that offered sufficient
darkness or reflective surfaces. Lucio Fontana was
one of the first to create light environments, and a
decade later one member of a commune-like movement, Group Zero in Germany, began a series of
works that introduced the added dimension of time
to light art. Otto Piene's works often took the form of
light performances that would exist for only the time
it took to present them. These manifestations and the
more object-oriented happenings occurred at about
the same time in the late 1950's.

This serigraph is from an album Piene has called
Rose or Star (Rose Oder Stern). In the concrete
poetry the artist has written to introduce the prints, he
contrasts the known limitations of form with the
limitless experience of perception. The prints are
meant to augment the range of perception of light
and intensify its contribution to human experience.
The outlines of the light image differ so that each
print in the album is an entity rather than an integral
part of a program of optical sensations. The artist
relates the pulsating black form in this serigraph to
the afterimage that the eye experiences after exposure to a very bright source of light.

Edward Ruscha   American, born 1937
Adios. 1969, Tamarind Lithography Workshop,
Los Angeles.
Color lithograph, 22-1/16 x 9-5/16″.
The Museum of Modern Art, New York (promised gift
of Kleiner, Bell & Co.).

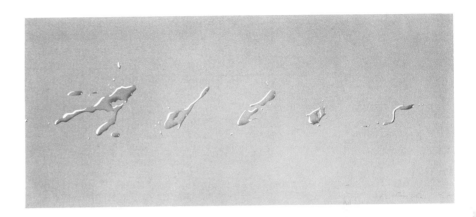

In their collages of ordinary commercial materials,
the cubists found a peculiar effectiveness in the
lettering that appeared on the labels and other
printed items. Often they would amputate parts of
words so that careful reading would reveal a pun.
The dada artists also used language to confuse the
obvious in their works. Abstract artists have continu-
ally incorporated letter signs into paintings, and
those artists who chose their images from popular
sources such as advertisements of necessity included trade names and emblems in their works
during the 1960's.

Edward Ruscha is an artist who lives in Los
Angeles, California, and has selected his imagery
from the manufactured landscape of the area. He has
depicted the monumental letters that spell out Holly-
wood on the hill above the city, and has compiled
photographs of twenty-six gasoline stations, thirty-
four parking lots, and other serial motifs that, in their
repetitive abundance, emphasize the artificial organization of human life. Ruscha avoids representing
people in his photographs and prints, but in his
compositions of single words the use in language of
such words is often personal and regional rather than
literary.

Adios is typical of Ruscha's work. The word is
executed as if it were liquid dripped onto the sheet.
Ruscha is also very interested in food and has
delighted in creating printing inks from caviar and
jam. He often conceives his works in the colors of
food, and *Adios* appears to be printed in Mexican
chili sauce. The word *adios* (goodbye, Spanish) is
quite commonly heard in Los Angeles, which has a
long Spanish history and where Mexicans form a
significant part of the community.

Gérard Titus-Carmel French, born 1942
Alteration of a Parallelipiped by Shifting. 1971.
Etching and drypoint, 16-5/16 x 20⅜".

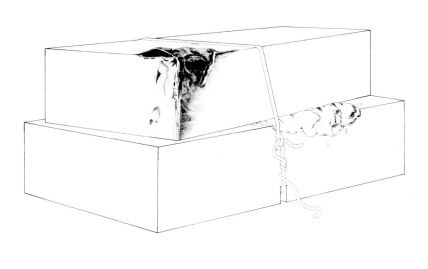

The young French artist Gérard Titus-Carmel is an inventor whose imagination exploits the unpredictability of incompatible materials. Like his scientific counterpart, the artist-inventor describes his experiments with the specialized language that makes abstruse its seemingly comprehensible appearance. In this print a soft substance appears to be pressed between two relatively hard, rectangular slabs, one of which has begun to deteriorate. It is a strange conjunction of materials, and the dry unemotional line of scientific illustration is one clue to the perception of the contrived construction. While the title characterizes what is depicted as a change in geometric form, emphasizing its abstract experimental quality, the visual elements evoke a sense of the voluptuous. The opposition of hard and soft and the disintegration of apparently stable matter are part of the artist's compendium of metaphors for life.

Titus-Carmel prefers to draw with pencil, and this drypoint is its intaglio equivalent. The artist draws his lines directly on the copper plate with a sharp point, either hard metal or one of several hard crystals such as diamond. The point creates a groove in the plate and the bits of copper it has dug up remain on the edges of the groove (burr). When the plate is inked, the burr holds some of the ink and when printed makes the line appear soft and furry.

Alena Kučerová   Czechoslovakian, born 1935
Shomeh. 1969.
Intaglio, 20-15/16 x 29⅞″.

Eastern Europe has offered more opportunities to
graphic artists, perhaps, than to painters and sculptors. In Poland and Yugoslavia important biennial
competitions have drawn the prints of the world's
major artists, and given the printmakers of those and
neighboring countries a broader understanding of
the great variety of currents and techniques being
exploited internationally. Far more portable than
paintings, prints by artists from Eastern European
countries are sent regularly to exhibitions in France,
Italy, Switzerland, and Japan. While the several
studios for printmakers in Paris still strongly influence
the younger artists who are able to leave their own
countries to attend them, many more have benefited
from fresh observations of their own traditional forms
and crafts made acute by the experience of seeing
the widest range of contemporary creativity.

The unusual quality of this landscape by the Czech
artist Alena Kučerová derives from a unique technique as well as an older tradition. The dotted con-
tour of the trees and land is made by perforating a
tin-coated metal sheet with puncturing tools. The
rough edges of the perforations only slightly catch
the ink rubbed onto the plate, making the dots stand
in white relief against an indefinite ground. The
dotted pattern recalls some motifs on Czech punched
leather work and bronze decorations.

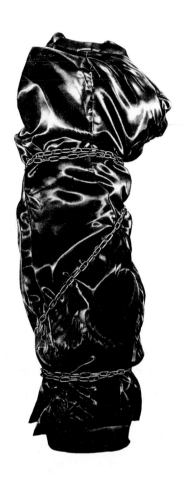

Wolfgang Gäfgen   German, born 1936
Mezzotint No. 2. (1972), Soleil Noir, Paris.
Mezzotint, 24-11/16 x 20-13/16".

The technique of mezzotint was invented in the seventeenth century. The French call it *manière noir* because the printmaker works from dark to light. A metal plate is abraded or stippled by a multitoothed tool called a rocker. To create an image within this area, the artist smooths down the pits and burrs by scraping and burnishing. When the plate is inked, the burrs hold the ink while the smoothed areas and lines are wiped clean. In the finished print solid mezzotint passages appear to have a soft, velvety texture.

The young German artist Wolfgang Gäfgen has specialized in the mezzotint technique. Yozo Hamaguchi and Mario Avati, the two best known twentieth-century mezzotint printmakers, are devoted to still-life representation. Gäfgen is also concerned with objects but only as ambiguous forms that might convey emotion. The satin-lined overcoat, bound with chains, is both fetishistic and human, its metaphoric content simultaneously mysterious and cruel, and its surface utterly sensuous. The isolation of one object was, during the period of pop art, largely a means of using contemporary images to create changes in two-dimensional composition. Gäfgen's meticulously detailed rendering of one ambivalent object microscopically examines and radically evaluates reality.

Gerd Winner   German, born 1936
Slow. (1972), Kelpra Studios, London.
Color serigraph, 24¾ x 24⅜".

Loneliness is dominant in the works of the realist artists who emerged during the last years of the 1960's. Those paintings and prints which present a frozen moment in human action are either nostalgic or anticipatory. Most human groups consist of separate persons involved in their own selves, even in the most intimate relationships. In compositions where the human being is absent the manufactured discomfort of the environment magnifies a sense of loss. By the method of instantaneous preservation of a moment of action or a static scene, the mechanism of photography, the new realist artists eliminate the continuity that is essential to human relationships with other human beings or with their environments. In order to reinforce the atmosphere of discontinued time and space, subjects are generally chosen from the period of the artist's childhood or show familiar places through which people pass without noticing. In the latter case the removal of the human element focuses attention on the individual details of the aesthetically torpid environment they have created for themselves.

The German artist Gerd Winner has taken the dingy gray permeated landscapes of London and focused attention on uninhabited wharf buildings and walled thoroughfares. In the screenprint *Slow* the man-devised traffic direction in an area seemingly devoid of human habitation or visitation ironically emphasizes the loss of this warning element in our lives. Winner takes a photograph, enlarges it, and screenprints it in black. The atmospheric colors as well as the disruptive street sign "Slow" are additional screens in which the color is printed flatly.

Care and Preservation of Prints
by Antoinette King

A print made only a short time ago can be in bad condition because of faulty framing, handling, and storage, or use of poor materials by the artist. That a print is damaged or deteriorated may be immediately apparent, but the causes are not always understood. The following pages will be a brief explanation of common damaging factors and their prevention.

Damaging Factors

Matboards. One of the most destructive things you can do to a print is to back it with cardboard. Unfortunately, most framers, past and present, with a few outstanding exceptions, use cardboard of various types to mat and mount prints. The cardboard can be of the gray, orange, or corrugated varieties. Ordinary cardboards are made primarily of ground wood pulp and contain acids that weaken any papers they are in contact with by causing breakdowns in the cellulose chains that make up the paper fibers. Cardboards also contain impurities and coloring matter that weaken and stain papers (see Fig. 1). Thus, for example, the brown lines from contact with corrugated cardboard can clearly be seen on the back of a print and, in time, work themselves to the front. Cardboard mats leave a brown stain all around the edges of the print.

Sometimes it is hard to tell poor-quality cardboard because it is surfaced with good-grade paper. In most instances you can identify the covered board by looking at the edge to see if the interior is the same color as the surface. Good-quality matboards have the same color and texture all the way through. When a window opening is cut in a paper-surfaced cardboard mat, the poor-quality pulp is exposed. Impurities in this pulp come in contact with the print and will stain it.

Tapes and Adhesives. The use of improper tapes and adhesives has ruined many works of art. Prints are frequently held to mounts or mats with gummed paper tape or pressure-sensitive tape. Gummed tapes leave yellow stains which can be difficult to remove on delicate papers. Pressure-sensitive tapes are made with an adhesive that exudes into the paper, causing a deep brown stain which can some-times be removed only partially, or not at all (see Fig. 2).

An adhesive tape all around the window opening of a linen or silk mat is a very popular look today. This particular adhesive tape stains the print very rapidly (see Fig. 3). Do not use mats of this type.

Often prints are glued to mounts at the corners, or all around the edges, with rubber cement, white glue, or any of a wide range of contemporary commercial adhesives all of which stain and damage paper. Manufacturers of these products do not recommend their use on works of art. Rubber cement and white glue are particularly difficult, and often impossible, to remove.

Light. The action of light is one of the most potent factors causing the deterioration of works of art. All wavelengths of light are damaging to paper, sizing, and many modern dyes and pigments. The damaging effects are cumulative. Low intensities of illumination for a long time can equal high intensities for a short time. Of course, the life of the object is shorter at high intensities.

Ultraviolet wavelengths are the most damaging. Direct sunlight and ordinary fluorescent lights have the highest proportion of ultraviolet and, if possible, should never be used for illuminating art. Indirect daylight also contains ultraviolet rays. If fluorescent lights are already present in a lighting system, they should have ultraviolet filters put over them; these are transparent plastic tubes accurately engineered to fit all sizes of fluorescent tubes. Incandescent lights have only a trace of ultraviolet, and are therefore the recommended light source.

The amount of visible light falling on a print can be measured very simply with a common light meter that is calibrated in footcandles. Extensive studies have shown the proper range of illumination for works of art to be from five to fifteen footcandles.

Small lights attached to the top of a frame are injurious. They direct an intense amount of light right next to the picture. Sometimes they give off enough heat to scorch the picture.

Light can bleach certain kinds of paper, but the usual visual effect is to yellow it; the darkening

Fig. 1. Verso of a print that was mounted on an orange cardboard.

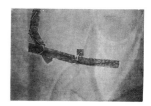
Fig. 2. Stain made by pressure-sensitive tape.

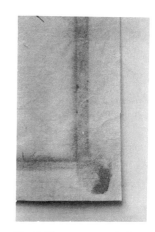
Fig. 3. The narrow stain is made by adhesive tape; the blob at the corner is from rubber cement.

Fig. 4. Stains made by mold growths.

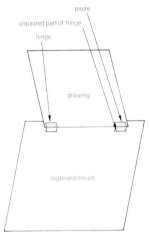

Fig. 5. Technique of applying a hinge.

ranges from light yellow to dark brown, depending on the extent of exposure and the type of paper. Many modern inks, dyes, and pigments are faded or darkened by light.

Relative Humidity and Temperature. Prints should be stored or hung at a temperature comfortable for people, between 68° and 70°F. The relative humidity should be 50% ± 10%. If the relative humidity is below 30% for long periods of time, paper loses necessary moisture irretrievably and becomes brittle. If the relative humidity goes above 70% there is danger of mold.

Mold. Mold spores are always present in the air and on objects. Under humid conditions mold can grow very rapidly on pictures. Ordinary mold growths leave a roundish, irregular stain varying in size (see Fig. 4). Sometimes tiny, rather regular, brown stains appear. Commonly called "foxing," they are caused by the action of mold on traces of iron salts in the paper.

Air Pollution. As everyone knows, the air in metropolitan areas today is very polluted. Certain components of this pollution, such as oxides of nitrogen and sulphur dioxide, are extremely harmful to works of art. These pollutants can convert to acids when in contact with paper. The breakdown of the paper from the action of acids can result in discolorations. These discolorations are most commonly seen on prints with inadequately sealed frames. Contemporary frames, such as a sandwich of plexiglass and cardboard held together with metal clamps, or molded plexiglass, cannot be adequately sealed. Polluted air seeps in from the sides or the back, ultimately leaving brown streaks where it has passed.

Dirt is also a major component in air pollution. It penetrates poorly sealed frames, or the drawers where prints are stored, leaving gray streaks on the paper. As time goes on, the particles of dirt sink deeper into the paper, cutting into its fibers. This weakens the sheet.

General Care

FRAMING. Matboard. The best material to use is 100% ragboard, which is made from strong cotton fibers. This board comes in a range of thicknesses, two-ply, four-ply, and eight-ply. Four-ply is generally recommended. Very large prints, or prints with collage or embossing, may need an eight-ply mat. Two four-ply boards can be used for the same purpose. Sometimes one of the boards is cut slightly smaller than the other to achieve a handsome presentation.

Hinging. The print is attached to a 100% ragboard mount with hinges of Japanese mulberry paper. The mulberry paper should be slightly lighter in weight than the paper support of the print. The adhesive to use is rice or wheat starch paste. Starch pastes do not discolor or harm the paper. The size of the hinge varies with the size of the print, but is usually ½ to 1½ inches long and ½ inch wide. If the print is small, two hinges are sufficient. If it is large, three or more are necessary.

The technique of applying the hinge is as follows: Rice or wheat starch paste, thinned with water, is brushed along the lower half of the hinge, leaving the outer edge unpasted— which facilitates removal of the hinge if necessary. Apply this half of the hinge to the print. Then place a small piece of smooth white blotter over it. Place a hard, flat surface, such as glass, over the blotter and weight it. Change the blotter after a few minutes, then leave it under weight for an hour or more until dry. Similarly, paste the other half of the hinge entirely and apply it to the mount (see Fig. 5).

Edges of the Print Covered with the Mat. In this case, a pendant type of hinge is used. If the print is large or heavy, an extra piece of mulberry paper is pasted across the part of the hinge on the rag mount to prevent slippage (see Fig. 6).

Edges of the Print Not Covered by the Mat, or "Floating." In this case, the print is hinged at the top, bottom, and sides to hold it flat and in place. The hinges are folded over so they don't show.

FRAME. Spacer. There is a danger that moisture will condense on the print surface if it presses against the glass or plexiglass. Also, if delicate matte-printed surfaces rub against glass or plexiglass, they can acquire an uneven shine. Therefore, if the print is "floated" without a window mat, or is oversize and consequently likely to buckle somewhat, the frame will need to be constructed with a spacer around the inner edge of the rabbet (see Fig. 8). The spacer should provide adequate depth to prevent the print from touching the glass or plexiglass.

Glass or Plexiglass. Plexiglass that has been scientifically developed to filter out harmful ultraviolet rays should be used in framing prints whenever possible. The grade of plexiglass that screens out almost 95% of the rays has a slight yellow tinge. Plexiglass that filters out about 90% of the rays and is colorless is also manufactured. A strong word of caution, however: Plexiglass causes static electricity and should *never* be used on a print if it has freestanding collage, or charcoal or pastel notations, which can be loosened and pulled off by this charge.

Backing. The final backing can be 100% ragboard or a strong, purified wood pulp board. Cheap cardboard is not recommended even for the outside of the frame because it becomes brittle and offers little protection against hard knocks; also, as it deteriorates, it stains and damages the ragboard mount.

Sealing. The back of the frame should be sealed against the penetration of dust with a wide tape, preferably a linen tape with water-soluble gum.

Storage. Areas where prints are stored or hung should be air-conditioned and kept at a constant relative humidity. If optimum controls are not possible, at least guarding against extremes will be beneficial. In dry climates, humidifiers will help to keep the relative humidity above 40%. In wet climates, dehumidifiers will keep the relative humidity below 70%. A simple method of determining the relative humidity of a room is to place a humidity-indicating paper in a central area. This indicator will change color with a change in relative humidity.

Dirt may be reduced with air filters. Shelves and cupboards should be vacuumed regularly.

Prints which are not being exhibited should be correctly matted in standard-size mats and stored flat in dustproof boxes made of acid-free material or in closed drawers or cupboards. Smooth, thin, good-quality, non-acid paper, such as a fine Japanese

mulberry paper, should be laid over the print surface to protect it.

General Handling. The surfaces of contemporary prints are particularly liable to damage. Even light fingermarks or slight scratches on the surface of a smooth serigraph can alter its appearance drastically; there is little that can be done to restore such a surface once it has been damaged. Thus, it is especially important to protect surfaces, and handle and carry prints with care. Smooth, thin non-acid paper laid gently on the surface of the print will protect it. Always have a good support, such as fresh cardboard, under a print when lifting or carrying it. Carrying an inadequately supported print risks creasing and tearing.

Conservation. If a print is damaged it must be sent to a conservator who specializes in paper preservation. Only a conservator with years of recognized training and experience should treat prints. A number of museums are prepared to provide names of trained conservators.

Note. Books listed in the ''Care and Preservation'' section of the Bibliography indicate sources for the materials required for mounting and protecting prints. In addition, the Conservation Department in many museums is authorized to give specific recommendations in response to inquiries about materials.

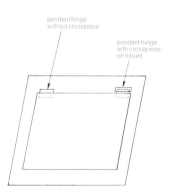

Fig. 6. Reinforced pendant-type hinge.

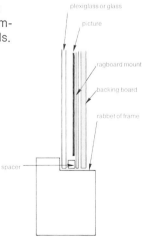

Fig. 7. Construction of frame with a spacer around the inner edge of the rabbet.

Selected Bibliography

General History

Gilmour, Pat. *Modern Prints.* New York, Studio Vista/Dutton, 1970.

Hayter, Stanley William. *About Prints.* London, Oxford University Press, 1962.

Johnson, Elaine L. *Contemporary Painters and Sculptors as Printmakers.* New York, The Museum of Modern Art, 1966.

Johnson, Una E. *Ten Years of American Prints: 1947–1956.* New York, Brooklyn Museum, 1956.

Man, Felix H. *Artist's Lithographs.* New York, H. Putnam, 1969.

Passeron, Roger. *French Prints of the 20th Century.* New York, Praeger, 1970.

Platt, Hans. *Artist's Prints in Colour.* London, Barrie and Rockliff, 1961.

Stubbe, Wolf. *Graphic Arts in the Twentieth Century.* New York, Praeger, 1963.

Weber, Wilhelm. *A History of Lithography.* New York, McGraw-Hill, 1966.

Zigrosser, Carl. *The Appeal of Prints.* Philadelphia, Leary's Co., 1970.

Techniques

Antreasian, Garo Z., with Adams, Clinton. *The Tamarind Book of Lithography: Art and Techniques.* New York, Harry N. Abrams, 1971.

Brunner, Felix. *A Handbook of Graphic Reproduction Processes.* New York, Hastings, 1962.

Daniels, Harvey. *Printmaking.* New York, Viking, 1971.

Hayter, Stanley William. *New Ways of Gravure.* London, Oxford University Press, 1966.

Heller, Jules. *Printmaking Today: A Studio Handbook.* New York, Holt, Rinehart and Winston, 1972.

Peterdi, Gabor. *Printmaking Methods Old and New.* New York, The MacMillan Co., 1971.

Rothenstein, Michael. *Relief Printing.* New York, Watson-Guptill, 1970.

Zigrosser, Carl, and Gaehde, Christa M. *A Guide to the Collecting and Care of Original Prints.* New York, Crown Publishers, Inc., 1966.

Care and Preservation

Control of the Museum Environment, A Basic Summary. International Institute for Conservation of Historic and Artistic Works, 608 Grand Buildings, Trafalgar Square, London, W.C. 2N, England, 1967.

Dolloff, Francis W., and Perkinson, Roy L. *How to Care for Works of Art on Paper,* Boston, Museum of Fine Arts, 1971.

Feller, Robert L. "Control of Deteriorating Effects of Light upon Museum Objects," *Museum,* Vol. XVII, No. 2, 1964.

Glaser, Mary Todd. *Framing & Preservation of Works of Art on Paper.* New York, Parke-Bernet Galleries, 1971.

Weidner, Marilyn Kemp. "Damage and Deterioration of Art on Paper Due to Ignorance and the Use of Faulty Materials," *Studies in Conservation,* Vol. 12, No. 1. n. d.

Zigrosser, Carl, and Gaehde, Christa M. *A Guide to the Collecting and Care of Original Prints,* New York, Crown Publishers, Inc., 1966.

Index